# POWER CUT

T0372655

by Peter Millett
illustrated by Russ Daff

CAMBRIDGE
UNIVERSITY PRESS

Institute of Education

# Chapter 1

It was an evening just like any other in the Chen family apartment.

Mr and Mrs Chen were tired from working all day, and the children were busy playing on tablets.

'Mum, can you play a game with me now?'
said Amy.

'Dad, do you want to play battleships?'
asked Ben.

Suddenly, the lights went off.

The apartment went completely dark.

'Oh no! We have lost all our electricity,' cried Mr Chen.

'There must be a power cut in the city,' said Mrs Chen.

## Chapter 2

'Is everybody okay?' asked Mr Chen.

'Yes, I'm okay,' said Amy.

'Wow! It's so dark in here,' said Ben.

'I've never seen our house like this before.'

Mr Chen picked up his torch and turned it on.

But there was only a small beam of light.

'Oh no,' groaned Mr Chen. 'The batteries in this torch are not very good.

I don't know how long this torchlight will last.'

The Chen family looked out of their apartment window.

Mrs Chen pointed at the sky. 'Look at all the stars.'

'Wow! I can see so many,' said Ben.

Then Mrs Chen wiped her forehead.

'I'm feeling very hot,' she said.

'So am I,' said Amy.

'Who turned the heater on?'

Mr Chen frowned.
'The heater is not on.

The machine that keeps us cool has stopped working.'

Mrs Chen went into the kitchen.

'Oh no! The fridge is not working either,' she cried. 'All the food will be ruined.'

'And what about the freezer?' asked Ben.

'The ice cream cake for Grandma is in there. It's a special treat for her.'

## Chapter 3

'That's a big problem,' said Amy.
'The ice cream cake will melt if it gets warm.'

Just then, the torch went out.

'And now we have an even bigger problem,' said Mr Chen.

'Oh dear. What do we do now?'
Mrs Chen asked.

Amy saw her tablet glowing in the corner
of the room.

'I have an idea,' she said.

She picked up her tablet and took it back into the kitchen.

'This tablet light will last for a few hours,' she said. 'Luckily, I charged it up this morning.'

'What a clever idea!' said Mr Chen.

'But what do we do about Grandma's melting ice cream cake?' he asked.

'I can fix that problem!' said Ben.

The tablet gave enough light for Mrs Chen
to put the ice cream cake into bowls
and find some spoons.

'I'm sure Grandma won't mind us eating it,' said Ben.

So the Chen family ate the cake and looked out of the window at the stars.

# Chapter 4

When they had finished eating, the Chen family played a game counting the big stars in the sky.

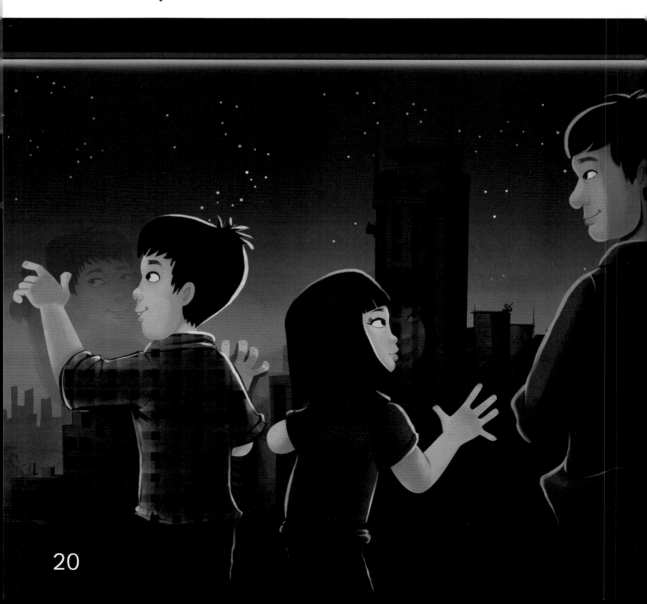

'This is so much fun,' said Ben. 'Can we do it again next time we have a power cut?'

'Of course we can,' laughed Mr Chen.

An hour later, the power came back on.

The apartment started to cool down
and the fridge began to work again.

'All our problems are solved,' said Mr Chen.

'But we still have one problem,'
laughed Mrs Chen.

'Who is going to tell Grandma that we ate
her cake?'

# POWER CUT ● PETER MILLETT

Teaching notes written by Sue Bodman and Glen Franklin

## Using this book

### Developing reading comprehension

The Chen family are getting ready for their evening at home when there is a power cut. How they cope in the dark, without any light or power, is the subject of this story. The book is written in four short chapters to support sustained reading. Many children will have experienced a power cut, but it is important to establish their prior knowledge before read this book with them.

### Grammar and sentence structure

- The story is told predominantly through dialogue, demarcated by speech marks.

- Sentences are varied for effect, for example by using shorter sentences ('*I can fix that problem.*') or by adding adverbial words and phrases ('*just then*', '*luckily*').

### Word meaning and spelling

- Syllabification of longer words enables word study for spelling inflectional endings and words with suffixes.

- Verbs used in reporting clauses ('*groaned*', '*asked*') demonstrate character and support expressive reading.

### Curriculum links

*Science* – This book will lead to lots of science experiments! Children could investigate with different torches and look at how far the beam will shine, or how long the battery will last. Try making shadow puppets, or drawing silhouettes by projecting a project a beam of light onto large sheets of paper. Experiment with melting ice: how long will it take to melt if there is no power to the freezer?

*PSHE* – The Chens had to find a way to get by without electricity for a few hours. Explore things in the home or in school that use electricity to run. What would they have to do if there was a power cut? How might they prepare? How would they help others?

## Learning Outcomes

Children can:

- sustain meaning and comprehension over longer texts, summarising the key events

- note and use speech punctuation paying attention to reporting clauses to aid expressive, fluent reading

- read more complex words using appropriate strategies including known phonic knowledge and syllabification.

## A guided reading lesson

### Book Introduction

Give each child a copy of the book. Ask them to read the title and blurb quietly to themselves. Ask: *What is a power cut? Has this ever happened to you? What did you do?*

### Orientation

*This story is about the Chen family; Mum, Dad, Amy and Ben. They are getting ready for a night at home, when there is a power cut. I wonder what they will do …*

### Preparation

Pages 4 and 5: These pages introduce the power cut. Look at some of the longer words on this page ('*apartment*', *electricity*'). Explore the regular usage of the /ly/ suffix to denote adverbs ('*completely*', '*suddenly*').

Demonstrate how to summarise the events: *Now I'm going to summarise what happened in that first chapter. In this chapter, the Chen family were getting ready for an evening at home, when there was a power cut. Let's see what happened next.*

In pairs, have the children skim the pages of Chapter Two (pages 6 to 13) and summarise